MW01171057

Other Works

Moon Ritual Alchemy ~ A guide to creating Lunar
Rituals
ISBN #979-8-218-45927-7

World Fusion Plant Based Recipe Book
ISBN #978-0-578-68913-5

BLACK SWAN TEMPLE

Moon Ritual Alchemy Journal

Track your lunar rituals, align with the moon's magic, and manifest your dreams.

Heather Regal & Donny Regal

Edition #1
ISBN #979-8-218-46189-8
www.BlackSwanTemple.org

Cover, Illustrator and Book Designer - Samantha Bacon

IG - Black_Swan_Temple
FB - BlackSwanTemple

RITUAL JOURNAL WORKSHEET

Phase Name : Write the name of the lunar phase (New Moon/Full Moon/Other)

_____

Date : Note the date of the phase.

_____

Intentions : What do you intend to manifest or release? Write in affirmative "I am ...." statements.

_____
_____
_____
_____
_____
_____
_____
_____

Moon Phase Meaning : Write down the meanings and symbolism associated with this lunar phase.

_____
_____
_____
_____

Ritual Practice : Describe the rituals you performed during this phase. Include any meditations, or ceremonies you engaged in.

_____

_____

_____

_____

_____

_____

Reflections : Reflect on your experiences, lessons learned and takeaways. How did you feel during, before and after the ritual? Did you notice any shifts or changes in your energy? Reflect on your emotions, mood and physical state during this lunar phase. How did you feel emotionally, mentally, physically and spiritually? Did you notice any changes in your energy levels, sleep patterns, or overall health? Did you receive any guidance or messages from your intuition, dreams, or spiritual practice? Write down three things that you are grateful for.

_____

_____

_____

_____

_____

_____

_____

_____

_____

_____

Next Steps : What are your next steps? Set intentions for the next lunar cycle.

_____

_____

_____

_____

_____

_____

_____

_____

_____

_____

_____

Closing Blessings : Offer a blessing or affirmation to conclude your journal entry and sign it.

_____

_____

_____

_____

_____

_____

_____

CREATIVE INSPIRATIONS

"The moon is a reflection of your heart and its light is your guide." – Rumi

RITUAL JOURNAL WORKSHEET

Phase Name : Write the name of the lunar phase (New Moon/Full Moon/Other)

_____

Date : Note the date of the phase.

_____

Intentions : What do you intend to manifest or release? Write in affirmative "I am ...." statements.

_____

_____

_____

_____

_____

_____

_____

_____

_____

_____

Moon Phase Meaning : Write down the meanings and symbolism associated with this lunar phase.

_____

_____

_____

_____

_____

Ritual Practice : Describe the rituals you performed during this phase. Include any meditations, or ceremonies you engaged in.

_____

_____

_____

_____

_____

Reflections : Reflect on your experiences, lessons learned and takeaways. How did you feel during, before and after the ritual? Did you notice any shifts or changes in your energy? Reflect on your emotions, mood and physical state during this lunar phase. How did you feel emotionally, mentally, physically and spiritually? Did you notice any changes in your energy levels, sleep patterns, or overall health? Did you receive any guidance or messages from your intuition, dreams, or spiritual practice? Write down three things that you are grateful for.

_____

_____

_____

_____

_____

_____

_____

_____

Next Steps : What are your next steps? Set intentions for the next lunar cycle.

_____

_____

_____

_____

_____

_____

_____

_____

_____

_____

_____

_____

Closing Blessings : Offer a blessing or affirmation to conclude your journal entry and sign it.

_____

_____

_____

_____

_____

_____

_____

CREATIVE
INSPIRATIONS

"As the moon knows, it's the quiet energy that has the power to pull."

RITUAL JOURNAL WORKSHEET

Phase Name : Write the name of the lunar phase (New Moon/Full Moon/Other)

_____

Date : Note the date of the phase.

_____

Intentions : What do you intend to manifest or release? Write in affirmative "I am ...." statements.

_____

_____

_____

_____

_____

_____

_____

_____

Moon Phase Meaning : Write down the meanings and symbolism associated with this lunar phase.

_____

_____

_____

_____

Ritual Practice : Describe the rituals you performed during this phase. Include any meditations, or ceremonies you engaged in.

_____

_____

_____

_____

_____

_____

Reflections : Reflect on your experiences, lessons learned and takeaways. How did you feel during, before and after the ritual? Did you notice any shifts or changes in your energy? Reflect on your emotions, mood and physical state during this lunar phase. How did you feel emotionally, mentally, physically and spiritually? Did you notice any changes in your energy levels, sleep patterns, or overall health? Did you receive any guidance or messages from your intuition, dreams, or spiritual practice? Write down three things that you are grateful for.

_____

_____

_____

_____

_____

_____

_____

_____

_____

Next Steps : What are your next steps? Set intentions for the next lunar cycle.

_____
_____
_____
_____
_____
_____
_____
_____
_____
_____
_____
_____

Closing Blessings : Offer a blessing or affirmation to conclude your journal entry and sign it.

_____
_____
_____
_____
_____
_____
_____

CREATIVE
INSPIRATIONS

"The moon is a reminder that no matter what phase you are in, you are still whole."

RITUAL JOURNAL WORKSHEET

Phase Name : Write the name of the lunar phase (New Moon/Full Moon/Other)

Date : Note the date of the phase.

Intentions : What do you intend to manifest or release? Write in affirmative "I am ...." statements.

Moon Phase Meaning : Write down the meanings and symbolism associated with this lunar phase.

Ritual Practice : Describe the rituals you performed during this phase. Include any meditations, or ceremonies you engaged in.

_____

_____

_____

_____

_____

_____

Reflections : Reflect on your experiences, lessons learned and takeaways. How did you feel during, before and after the ritual? Did you notice any shifts or changes in your energy? Reflect on your emotions, mood and physical state during this lunar phase. How did you feel emotionally, mentally, physically and spiritually? Did you notice any changes in your energy levels, sleep patterns, or overall health? Did you receive any guidance or messages from your intuition, dreams, or spiritual practice? Write down three things that you are grateful for.

_____

_____

_____

_____

_____

_____

_____

_____

_____

Next Steps : What are your next steps? Set intentions for the next lunar cycle.

_____

_____

_____

_____

_____

_____

_____

_____

_____

_____

_____

Closing Blessings : Offer a blessing or affirmation to conclude your journal entry and sign it.

_____

_____

_____

_____

_____

_____

_____

_____

CREATIVE
INSPIRATIONS

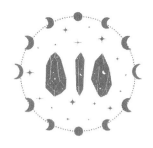

"Just like the moon, we go through phases of light and dark, and that's okay."

RITUAL JOURNAL WORKSHEET

Phase Name : Write the name of the lunar phase (New Moon/Full Moon/Other)

_____

Date : Note the date of the phase.

_____

Intentions : What do you intend to manifest or release? Write in affirmative "I am ...." statements.

_____

_____

_____

_____

_____

_____

_____

_____

_____

Moon Phase Meaning : Write down the meanings and symbolism associated with this lunar phase.

_____

_____

_____

_____

Ritual Practice : Describe the rituals you performed during this phase. Include any meditations, or ceremonies you engaged in.

_____

_____

_____

_____

_____

Reflections : Reflect on your experiences, lessons learned and takeaways. How did you feel during, before and after the ritual? Did you notice any shifts or changes in your energy? Reflect on your emotions, mood and physical state during this lunar phase. How did you feel emotionally, mentally, physically and spiritually? Did you notice any changes in your energy levels, sleep patterns, or overall health? Did you receive any guidance or messages from your intuition, dreams, or spiritual practice? Write down three things that you are grateful for.

_____

_____

_____

_____

_____

_____

_____

_____

_____

Next Steps : What are your next steps? Set intentions for the next lunar cycle.

_____
_____
_____
_____
_____
_____
_____
_____
_____
_____
_____
_____

Closing Blessings : Offer a blessing or affirmation to conclude your journal entry and sign it.

_____
_____
_____
_____
_____
_____
_____

CREATIVE
INSPIRATIONS

"The moon stays bright when it doesn't avoid the night." – Rumi

RITUAL JOURNAL WORKSHEET

Phase Name : Write the name of the lunar phase (New Moon/Full Moon/Other)

_____

Date : Note the date of the phase.

_____

Intentions : What do you intend to manifest or release? Write in affirmative "I am ...." statements.

_____
_____
_____
_____
_____
_____
_____
_____

Moon Phase Meaning : Write down the meanings and symbolism associated with the lunar phase.

_____
_____
_____
_____

Ritual Practice : Describe the rituals you performed during this phase. Include any meditations, or ceremonies you engaged in.

_____

_____

_____

_____

_____

_____

Reflections : Reflect on your experiences, lessons learned and takeaways. How did you feel during, before and after the ritual? Did you notice any shifts or changes in your energy? Reflect on your emotions, mood and physical state during this lunar phase. How did you feel emotionally, mentally, physically and spiritually? Did you notice any changes in your energy levels, sleep patterns, or overall health? Did you receive any guidance or messages from your intuition, dreams, or spiritual practice? Write down three things that you are grateful for.

_____

_____

_____

_____

_____

_____

_____

_____

_____

Next Steps : What are your next steps? Set intentions for the next lunar cycle.

_____

_____

_____

_____

_____

_____

_____

_____

_____

_____

_____

_____

Closing Blessings : Offer a blessing or affirmation to conclude your journal entry and sign it.

_____

_____

_____

_____

_____

_____

_____

CREATIVE
INSPIRATIONS

"Let the magic of the moonlight guide your soul to a place of peace and harmony."

RITUAL JOURNAL WORKSHEET

Phase Name : Write the name of the lunar phase (New Moon/Full Moon/Other)

_____

Date : Note the date of the phase.

_____

Intentions : What do you intend to manifest or release? Write in affirmative "I am ...." statements.

_____

_____

_____

_____

_____

_____

_____

_____

_____

Moon Phase Meaning : Write down the meanings and symbolism associated with the lunar phase.

_____

_____

_____

_____

Ritual Practice : Describe the rituals you performed during this phase. Include any meditations, or ceremonies you engaged in.

_____

_____

_____

_____

_____

_____

Reflections : Reflect on your experiences, lessons learned and takeaways. How did you feel during, before and after the ritual? Did you notice any shifts or changes in your energy? Reflect on your emotions, mood and physical state during this lunar phase. How did you feel emotionally, mentally, physically and spiritually? Did you notice any changes in your energy levels, sleep patterns, or overall health? Did you receive any guidance or messages from your intuition, dreams, or spiritual practice? Write down three things that you are grateful for.

_____

_____

_____

_____

_____

_____

_____

_____

_____

_____

Next Steps : What are your next steps? Set intentions for the next lunar cycle.

_____

_____

_____

_____

_____

_____

_____

_____

_____

_____

_____

Closing Blessings : Offer a blessing or affirmation to conclude your journal entry and sign it.

_____

_____

_____

_____

_____

_____

_____

_____

CREATIVE
INSPIRATIONS

"The moon is a reminder that no matter what phase you are in, you are still whole."

RITUAL JOURNAL WORKSHEET

Phase Name : Write the name of the lunar phase (New Moon/Full Moon/Other)

_____

Date : Note the date of the phase.

_____

Intentions : What do you intend to manifest or release? Write in affirmative "I am ...." statements.

_____
_____
_____
_____
_____
_____
_____
_____
_____
_____
_____

Moon Phase Meaning : Write down the meanings and symbolism associated with the lunar phase.

_____
_____
_____
_____
_____

Ritual Practice : Describe the rituals you performed during this phase. Include any meditations, or ceremonies you engaged in.

_____

_____

_____

_____

_____

_____

Reflections : Reflect on your experiences, lessons learned and takeaways. How did you feel during, before and after the ritual? Did you notice any shifts or changes in your energy? Reflect on your emotions, mood and physical state during this lunar phase. How did you feel emotionally, mentally, physically and spiritually? Did you notice any changes in your energy levels, sleep patterns, or overall health? Did you receive any guidance or messages from your intuition, dreams, or spiritual practice? Write down three things that you are grateful for.

_____

_____

_____

_____

_____

_____

_____

_____

_____

Next Steps : What are your next steps? Set intentions for the next lunar cycle.

_____

_____

_____

_____

_____

_____

_____

_____

_____

_____

Closing Blessings : Offer a blessing or affirmation to conclude your journal entry and sign it.

_____

_____

_____

_____

_____

_____

_____

CREATIVE
INSPIRATIONS

"Every new moon is a new beginning; use it wisely."

RITUAL JOURNAL WORKSHEET

Phase Name : Write the name of the lunar phase (New Moon/Full Moon/Other)

_____

Date : Note the date of the phase.

_____

Intentions : What do you intend to manifest or release? Write in affirmative "I am ...." statements.

_____
_____
_____
_____
_____
_____
_____
_____
_____
_____

Moon Phase Meaning : Write down the meanings and symbolism associated with the lunar phase.

_____
_____
_____
_____

Ritual Practice : Describe the rituals you performed during this phase. Include any meditations, or ceremonies you engaged in.

Reflections : Reflect on your experiences, lessons learned and takeaways. How did you feel during, before and after the ritual? Did you notice any shifts or changes in your energy? Reflect on your emotions, mood and physical state during this lunar phase. How did you feel emotionally, mentally, physically and spiritually? Did you notice any changes in your energy levels, sleep patterns, or overall health? Did you receive any guidance or messages from your intuition, dreams, or spiritual practice? Write down three things that you are grateful for.

Next Steps : What are your next steps? Set intentions for the next lunar cycle.

_____

_____

_____

_____

_____

_____

_____

_____

_____

_____

_____

_____

_____

Closing Blessings : Offer a blessing or affirmation to conclude your journal entry and sign it.

_____

_____

_____

_____

_____

_____

_____

CREATIVE
INSPIRATIONS

"Just as the moon phases, so too do we. Embrace each phase and its unique gifts."

RITUAL JOURNAL WORKSHEET

Phase Name : Write the name of the lunar phase (New Moon/Full Moon/Other)

Date : Note the date of the phase.

Intentions : What do you intend to manifest or release? Write in affirmative "I am ...." statements.

Moon Phase Meaning : Write down the meanings and symbolism associated with the lunar phase.

Ritual Practice : Describe the rituals you performed during this phase. Include any meditations, or ceremonies you engaged in.

_____

_____

_____

_____

_____

Reflections : Reflect on your experiences, lessons learned and takeaways. How did you feel during, before and after the ritual? Did you notice any shifts or changes in your energy? Reflect on your emotions, mood and physical state during this lunar phase. How did you feel emotionally, mentally, physically and spiritually? Did you notice any changes in your energy levels, sleep patterns, or overall health? Did you receive any guidance or messages from your intuition, dreams, or spiritual practice? Write down three things that you are grateful for.

_____

_____

_____

_____

_____

_____

_____

_____

_____

Next Steps : What are your next steps? Set intentions for the next lunar cycle.

_____

_____

_____

_____

_____

_____

_____

_____

_____

_____

_____

Closing Blessings : Offer a blessing or affirmation to conclude your journal entry and sign it.

_____

_____

_____

_____

_____

_____

_____

CREATIVE INSPIRATIONS

"Under the light of the moon, let your spirit awaken and your dreams take flight."

RITUAL JOURNAL WORKSHEET

Phase Name : Write the name of the lunar phase (New Moon/Full Moon/Other)

_____

Date : Note the date of the phase.

_____

Intentions : What do you intend to manifest or release? Write in affirmative "I am ...." statements.

_____

_____

_____

_____

_____

_____

_____

_____

_____

_____

Moon Phase Meaning : Write down the meanings and symbolism associated with the lunar phase.

_____

_____

_____

_____

_____

Ritual Practice : Describe the rituals you performed during this phase. Include any meditations, or ceremonies you engaged in.

_____

_____

_____

_____

_____

_____

Reflections : Reflect on your experiences, lessons learned and takeaways. How did you feel during, before and after the ritual? Did you notice any shifts or changes in your energy? Reflect on your emotions, mood and physical state during this lunar phase. How did you feel emotionally, mentally, physically and spiritually? Did you notice any changes in your energy levels, sleep patterns, or overall health? Did you receive any guidance or messages from your intuition, dreams, or spiritual practice? Write down three things that you are grateful for.

_____

_____

_____

_____

_____

_____

_____

_____

_____

Next Steps : What are your next steps? Set intentions for the next lunar cycle.

_____

_____

_____

_____

_____

_____

_____

_____

_____

_____

_____

_____

Closing Blessings : Offer a blessing or affirmation to conclude your journal entry and sign it.

_____

_____

_____

_____

_____

_____

_____

CREATIVE
INSPIRATIONS

Just like the moon, we go through phases to reflect the light and the darkness within us."

RITUAL JOURNAL WORKSHEET

Phase Name : Write the name of the lunar phase (New Moon/Full Moon/Other)

_____

Date : Note the date of the phase.

_____

Intentions : What do you intend to manifest or release? Write in affirmative "I am ...." statements.

_____
_____
_____
_____
_____
_____
_____
_____
_____
_____

Moon Phase Meaning : Write down the meanings and symbolism associated with the lunar phase.

_____
_____
_____
_____

Ritual Practice : Describe the rituals you performed during this phase. Include any meditations, or ceremonies you engaged in.

_____

_____

_____

_____

_____

_____

Reflections : Reflect on your experiences, lessons learned and takeaways. How did you feel during, before and after the ritual? Did you notice any shifts or changes in your energy? Reflect on your emotions, mood and physical state during this lunar phase. How did you feel emotionally, mentally, physically and spiritually? Did you notice any changes in your energy levels, sleep patterns, or overall health? Did you receive any guidance or messages from your intuition, dreams, or spiritual practice? Write down three things that you are grateful for.

_____

_____

_____

_____

_____

_____

_____

_____

_____

Next Steps : What are your next steps? Set intentions for the next lunar cycle.

_____

_____

_____

_____

_____

_____

_____

_____

_____

_____

_____

Closing Blessings : Offer a blessing or affirmation to conclude your journal entry and sign it.

_____

_____

_____

_____

_____

_____

_____

CREATIVE
INSPIRATIONS

"As the moon knows, it's the quiet energy that has the power to pull."

RITUAL JOURNAL WORKSHEET

Phase Name : Write the name of the lunar phase (New Moon/Full Moon/Other)

Date : Note the date of the phase.

Intentions : What do you intend to manifest or release? Write in affirmative "I am ...." statements.

Moon Phase Meaning : Write down the meanings and symbolism associated with the lunar phase.

Ritual Practice : Describe the rituals you performed during this phase. Include any meditations, or ceremonies you engaged in.

_____

_____

_____

_____

_____

_____

Reflections : Reflect on your experiences, lessons learned and takeaways. How did you feel during, before and after the ritual? Did you notice any shifts or changes in your energy? Reflect on your emotions, mood and physical state during this lunar phase. How did you feel emotionally, mentally, physically and spiritually? Did you notice any changes in your energy levels, sleep patterns, or overall health? Did you receive any guidance or messages from your intuition, dreams, or spiritual practice? Write down three things that you are grateful for.

_____

_____

_____

_____

_____

_____

_____

_____

_____

_____

Next Steps : What are your next steps? Set intentions for the next lunar cycle.

_____

_____

_____

_____

_____

_____

_____

_____

_____

_____

_____

_____

_____

_____

Closing Blessings : Offer a blessing or affirmation to conclude your journal entry and sign it.

_____

_____

_____

_____

_____

_____

_____

_____

CREATIVE INSPIRATIONS

"The moon is a reflection of your heart and its light is your guide." — Rumi

RITUAL JOURNAL WORKSHEET

Phase Name : Write the name of the lunar phase (New Moon/Full Moon/Other)

_____

Date : Note the date of the phase.

_____

Intentions : What do you intend to manifest or release? Write in affirmative "I am ...." statements.

_____

_____

_____

_____

_____

_____

_____

_____

_____

Moon Phase Meaning : Write down the meanings and symbolism associated with the lunar phase.

_____

_____

_____

_____

Ritual Practice : Describe the rituals you performed during this phase. Include any meditations, or ceremonies you engaged in.

_____

_____

_____

_____

_____

_____

Reflections : Reflect on your experiences, lessons learned and takeaways. How did you feel during, before and after the ritual? Did you notice any shifts or changes in your energy? Reflect on your emotions, mood and physical state during this lunar phase. How did you feel emotionally, mentally, physically and spiritually? Did you notice any changes in your energy levels, sleep patterns, or overall health? Did you receive any guidance or messages from your intuition, dreams, or spiritual practice? Write down three things that you are grateful for.

_____

_____

_____

_____

_____

_____

_____

_____

_____

_____

_____

Next Steps : What are your next steps? Set intentions for the next lunar cycle.

_____

_____

_____

_____

_____

_____

_____

_____

_____

_____

_____

_____

Closing Blessings : Offer a blessing or affirmation to conclude your journal entry and sign it.

_____

_____

_____

_____

_____

_____

_____

CREATIVE INSPIRATIONS

"As the moon knows, it's the quiet energy that has the power to pull."

RITUAL JOURNAL WORKSHEET

Phase Name : Write the name of the lunar phase (New Moon/Full Moon/Other)

_____

Date : Note the date of the phase.

_____

Intentions : What do you intend to manifest or release? Write in affirmative "I am ...." statements.

_____

_____

_____

_____

_____

_____

_____

_____

_____

Moon Phase Meaning : Write down the meanings and symbolism associated with the lunar phase.

_____

_____

_____

_____

Ritual Practice : Describe the rituals you performed during this phase. Include any meditations, or ceremonies you engaged in.

_____

_____

_____

_____

_____

_____

Reflections : Reflect on your experiences, lessons learned and takeaways. How did you feel during, before and after the ritual? Did you notice any shifts or changes in your energy? Reflect on your emotions, mood and physical state during this lunar phase. How did you feel emotionally, mentally, physically and spiritually? Did you notice any changes in your energy levels, sleep patterns, or overall health? Did you receive any guidance or messages from your intuition, dreams, or spiritual practice? Write down three things that you are grateful for.

_____

_____

_____

_____

_____

_____

_____

_____

_____

_____

Next Steps : What are your next steps? Set intentions for the next lunar cycle.

_____

_____

_____

_____

_____

_____

_____

_____

_____

_____

_____

_____

Closing Blessings : Offer a blessing or affirmation to conclude your journal entry and sign it.

_____

_____

_____

_____

_____

_____

_____

CREATIVE
INSPIRATIONS

"The moon is a reminder that no matter what phase you are in, you are still whole."

RITUAL JOURNAL WORKSHEET

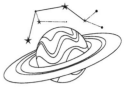

Phase Name : Write the name of the lunar phase (New Moon/Full Moon/Other)

_____

Date : Note the date of the phase.

_____

Intentions : What do you intend to manifest or release? Write in affirmative "I am ...." statements.

_____
_____
_____
_____
_____
_____
_____
_____
_____

Moon Phase Meaning : Write down the meanings and symbolism associated with the lunar phase.

_____
_____
_____
_____

Ritual Practice : Describe the rituals you performed during this phase. Include any meditations, or ceremonies you engaged in.

_____

_____

_____

_____

_____

_____

Reflections : Reflect on your experiences, lessons learned and takeaways. How did you feel during, before and after the ritual? Did you notice any shifts or changes in your energy? Reflect on your emotions, mood and physical state during this lunar phase. How did you feel emotionally, mentally, physically and spiritually? Did you notice any changes in your energy levels, sleep patterns, or overall health? Did you receive any guidance or messages from your intuition, dreams, or spiritual practice? Write down three things that you are grateful for.

_____

_____

_____

_____

_____

_____

_____

_____

_____

_____

Next Steps : What are your next steps? Set intentions for the next
lunar cycle.

_____

_____

_____

_____

_____

_____

_____

_____

_____

_____

_____

_____

Closing Blessings : Offer a blessing or affirmation to conclude your
journal entry and sign it.

_____

_____

_____

_____

_____

_____

_____

CREATIVE
INSPIRATIONS

"Just like the moon, we go through phases of light and dark, and that's okay."

RITUAL JOURNAL WORKSHEET

Phase Name : Write the name of the lunar phase (New Moon/Full Moon/Other)

Date : Note the date of the phase.

Intentions : What do you intend to manifest or release? Write in affirmative "I am ...." statements.

_____

_____

_____

_____

_____

_____

_____

_____

_____

Moon Phase Meaning : Write down the meanings and symbolism associated with the lunar phase.

_____

_____

_____

_____

Ritual Practice : Describe the rituals you performed during this phase. Include any meditations, or ceremonies you engaged in.

_____

_____

_____

_____

_____

_____

Reflections : Reflect on your experiences, lessons learned and takeaways. How did you feel during, before and after the ritual? Did you notice any shifts or changes in your energy? Reflect on your emotions, mood and physical state during this lunar phase. How did you feel emotionally, mentally, physically and spiritually? Did you notice any changes in your energy levels, sleep patterns, or overall health? Did you receive any guidance or messages from your intuition, dreams, or spiritual practice? Write down three things that you are grateful for.

_____

_____

_____

_____

_____

_____

_____

_____

_____

Next Steps : What are your next steps? Set intentions for the next lunar cycle.

_____

_____

_____

_____

_____

_____

_____

_____

_____

_____

Closing Blessings : Offer a blessing or affirmation to conclude your journal entry and sign it.

_____

_____

_____

_____

_____

_____

_____

CREATIVE INSPIRATIONS

"The moon stays bright when it doesn't avoid the night." – Rumi

RITUAL JOURNAL WORKSHEET

Phase Name : Write the name of the lunar phase (New Moon/Full Moon/Other)

_____

Date : Note the date of the phase.

_____

Intentions : What do you intend to manifest or release? Write in affirmative "I am ...." statements.

_____

_____

_____

_____

_____

_____

_____

_____

_____

Moon Phase Meaning : Write down the meanings and symbolism associated with the lunar phase.

_____

_____

_____

_____

_____

Ritual Practice : Describe the rituals you performed during this phase. Include any meditations, or ceremonies you engaged in.

_____

_____

_____

_____

_____

_____

Reflections : Reflect on your experiences, lessons learned and takeaways. How did you feel during, before and after the ritual? Did you notice any shifts or changes in your energy? Reflect on your emotions, mood and physical state during this lunar phase. How did you feel emotionally, mentally, physically and spiritually? Did you notice any changes in your energy levels, sleep patterns, or overall health? Did you receive any guidance or messages from your intuition, dreams, or spiritual practice? Write down three things that you are grateful for.

_____

_____

_____

_____

_____

_____

_____

_____

_____

Next Steps : What are your next steps? Set intentions for the next lunar cycle.

_____

_____

_____

_____

_____

_____

_____

_____

_____

_____

_____

_____

Closing Blessings : Offer a blessing or affirmation to conclude your journal entry and sign it.

_____

_____

_____

_____

_____

_____

_____

CREATIVE
INSPIRATIONS

"Let the magic of the moonlight guide your soul to a place of peace and harmony."

RITUAL JOURNAL WORKSHEET

Phase Name : Write the name of the lunar phase (New Moon/Full Moon/Other)

Date : Note the date of the phase.

Intentions : What do you intend to manifest or release? Write in affirmative "I am ...." statements.

Moon Phase Meaning : Write down the meanings and symbolism associated with the lunar phase.

Ritual Practice : Describe the rituals you performed during this phase. Include any meditations, or ceremonies you engaged in.

_____

_____

_____

_____

_____

_____

Reflections : Reflect on your experiences, lessons learned and takeaways. How did you feel during, before and after the ritual? Did you notice any shifts or changes in your energy? Reflect on your emotions, mood and physical state during this lunar phase. How did you feel emotionally, mentally, physically and spiritually? Did you notice any changes in your energy levels, sleep patterns, or overall health? Did you receive any guidance or messages from your intuition, dreams, or spiritual practice? Write down three things that you are grateful for.

_____

_____

_____

_____

_____

_____

_____

_____

_____

Next Steps : What are your next steps? Set intentions for the next lunar cycle.

_____

_____

_____

_____

_____

_____

_____

_____

_____

_____

_____

Closing Blessings : Offer a blessing or affirmation to conclude your journal entry and sign it.

_____

_____

_____

_____

_____

_____

_____

CREATIVE
INSPIRATIONS

"The moon is a reminder that no matter what phase you are in, you are still whole."

RITUAL JOURNAL WORKSHEET

Phase Name : Write the name of the lunar phase (New Moon/Full Moon/Other)

_____

Date : Note the date of the phase.

_____

Intentions : What do you intend to manifest or release? Write in affirmative "I am ...." statements.

_____

_____

_____

_____

_____

_____

_____

_____

_____

Moon Phase Meaning : Write down the meanings and symbolism associated with the lunar phase.

_____

_____

_____

_____

Ritual Practice : Describe the rituals you performed during this phase. Include any meditations, or ceremonies you engaged in.

_____

_____

_____

_____

_____

Reflections : Reflect on your experiences, lessons learned and takeaways. How did you feel during, before and after the ritual? Did you notice any shifts or changes in your energy? Reflect on your emotions, mood and physical state during this lunar phase. How did you feel emotionally, mentally, physically and spiritually? Did you notice any changes in your energy levels, sleep patterns, or overall health? Did you receive any guidance or messages from your intuition, dreams, or spiritual practice? Write down three things that you are grateful for.

_____

_____

_____

_____

_____

_____

_____

_____

_____

_____

Next Steps : What are your next steps? Set intentions for the next lunar cycle.

_____

_____

_____

_____

_____

_____

_____

_____

_____

_____

_____

_____

Closing Blessings : Offer a blessing or affirmation to conclude your journal entry and sign it.

_____

_____

_____

_____

_____

_____

_____

CREATIVE
INSPIRATIONS

"The moon is a reminder that no matter what phase you are in, you are still whole."

RITUAL JOURNAL WORKSHEET

Phase Name : Write the name of the lunar phase (New Moon/Full Moon/Other)

_____

Date : Note the date of the phase.

_____

Intentions : What do you intend to manifest or release? Write in affirmative "I am ...." statements.

_____

_____

_____

_____

_____

_____

_____

_____

_____

_____

Moon Phase Meaning : Write down the meanings and symbolism associated with the lunar phase.

_____

_____

_____

_____

Ritual Practice : Describe the rituals you performed during this phase. Include any meditations, or ceremonies you engaged in.

_____

_____

_____

_____

_____

_____

Reflections : Reflect on your experiences, lessons learned and takeaways. How did you feel during, before and after the ritual? Did you notice any shifts or changes in your energy? Reflect on your emotions, mood and physical state during this lunar phase. How did you feel emotionally, mentally, physically and spiritually? Did you notice any changes in your energy levels, sleep patterns, or overall health? Did you receive any guidance or messages from your intuition, dreams, or spiritual practice? Write down three things that you are grateful for.

_____

_____

_____

_____

_____

_____

_____

_____

_____

_____

Next Steps : What are your next steps? Set intentions for the next lunar cycle.

_____

_____

_____

_____

_____

_____

_____

_____

_____

_____

_____

Closing Blessings : Offer a blessing or affirmation to conclude your journal entry and sign it.

_____

_____

_____

_____

_____

_____

_____

_____

CREATIVE
INSPIRATIONS

"Every new moon is a new beginning; use it wisely."

RITUAL JOURNAL WORKSHEET

Phase Name : Write the name of the lunar phase (New Moon/Full Moon/Other)

_____

Date : Note the date of the phase.

_____

Intentions : What do you intend to manifest or release? Write in affirmative "I am ...." statements.

_____
_____
_____
_____
_____
_____
_____
_____
_____

Moon Phase Meaning : Write down the meanings and symbolism associated with the lunar phase.

_____
_____
_____
_____

Ritual Practice : Describe the rituals you performed during this phase. Include any meditations, or ceremonies you engaged in.

_____

_____

_____

_____

_____

Reflections : Reflect on your experiences, lessons learned and takeaways. How did you feel during, before and after the ritual? Did you notice any shifts or changes in your energy? Reflect on your emotions, mood and physical state during this lunar phase. How did you feel emotionally, mentally, physically and spiritually? Did you notice any changes in your energy levels, sleep patterns, or overall health? Did you receive any guidance or messages from your intuition, dreams, or spiritual practice? Write down three things that you are grateful for.

_____

_____

_____

_____

_____

_____

_____

_____

_____

_____

Aries

Next Steps : What are your next steps? Set intentions for the next lunar cycle.

_____

_____

_____

_____

_____

_____

_____

_____

_____

_____

_____

_____

Closing Blessings : Offer a blessing or affirmation to conclude your journal entry and sign it.

_____

_____

_____

_____

_____

_____

_____

CREATIVE
INSPIRATIONS

"Just as the moon phases, so too do we. Embrace each phase and its unique gifts."

RITUAL JOURNAL WORKSHEET

Phase Name : Write the name of the lunar phase (New Moon/Full Moon/Other)

Date : Note the date of the phase.

Intentions : What do you intend to manifest or release? Write in affirmative "I am ...." statements.

Moon Phase Meaning : Write down the meanings and symbolism associated with the lunar phase.

Ritual Practice : Describe the rituals you performed during this phase. Include any meditations, or ceremonies you engaged in.

_____

_____

_____

_____

_____

Reflections : Reflect on your experiences, lessons learned and takeaways. How did you feel during, before and after the ritual? Did you notice any shifts or changes in your energy? Reflect on your emotions, mood and physical state during this lunar phase. How did you feel emotionally, mentally, physically and spiritually? Did you notice any changes in your energy levels, sleep patterns, or overall health? Did you receive any guidance or messages from your intuition, dreams, or spiritual practice? Write down three things that you are grateful for.

_____

_____

_____

_____

_____

_____

_____

_____

_____

Next Steps : What are your next steps? Set intentions for the next lunar cycle.

_____

_____

_____

_____

_____

_____

_____

_____

_____

_____

_____

_____

Closing Blessings : Offer a blessing or affirmation to conclude your journal entry and sign it.

_____

_____

_____

_____

_____

_____

_____

CREATIVE
INSPIRATIONS

"The moon is a reflection of your heart and its light is your guide." — Rumi

RITUAL JOURNAL
WORKSHEET

Phase Name : Write the name of the lunar phase (New Moon/Full Moon/Other)

Date : Note the date of the phase.

Intentions : What do you intend to manifest or release? Write in affirmative "I am ...." statements.

Moon Phase Meaning : Write down the meanings and symbolism associated with the lunar phase.

Ritual Practice : Describe the rituals you performed during this phase. Include any meditations, or ceremonies you engaged in.

_____

_____

_____

_____

_____

_____

Reflections : Reflect on your experiences, lessons learned and takeaways. How did you feel during, before and after the ritual? Did you notice any shifts or changes in your energy? Reflect on your emotions, mood and physical state during this lunar phase. How did you feel emotionally, mentally, physically and spiritually? Did you notice any changes in your energy levels, sleep patterns, or overall health? Did you receive any guidance or messages from your intuition, dreams, or spiritual practice? Write down three things that you are grateful for.

_____

_____

_____

_____

_____

_____

_____

_____

Next Steps : What are your next steps? Set intentions for the next lunar cycle.

_____

_____

_____

_____

_____

_____

_____

_____

_____

_____

_____

_____

Closing Blessings : Offer a blessing or affirmation to conclude your journal entry and sign it.

_____

_____

_____

_____

_____

_____

_____

CREATIVE
INSPIRATIONS

"Under the light of the moon, let your spirit awaken and your dreams take flight."

RITUAL JOURNAL WORKSHEET

Phase Name : Write the name of the lunar phase (New Moon/Full Moon/Other)

_____

Date : Note the date of the phase.

_____

Intentions : What do you intend to manifest or release? Write in affirmative "I am ...." statements.

_____

_____

_____

_____

_____

_____

_____

_____

_____

Moon Phase Meaning : Write down the meanings and symbolism associated with the lunar phase.

_____

_____

_____

_____

Ritual Practice : Describe the rituals you performed during this phase. Include any meditations, or ceremonies you engaged in.

_____

_____

_____

_____

_____

Reflections : Reflect on your experiences, lessons learned and takeaways. How did you feel during, before and after the ritual? Did you notice any shifts or changes in your energy? Reflect on your emotions, mood and physical state during this lunar phase. How did you feel emotionally, mentally, physically and spiritually? Did you notice any changes in your energy levels, sleep patterns, or overall health? Did you receive any guidance or messages from your intuition, dreams, or spiritual practice? Write down three things that you are grateful for.

_____

_____

_____

_____

_____

_____

_____

_____

_____

Next Steps : What are your next steps? Set intentions for the next lunar cycle.

_____
_____
_____
_____
_____
_____
_____
_____
_____
_____
_____

Closing Blessings : Offer a blessing or affirmation to conclude your journal entry and sign it.

_____
_____
_____
_____
_____
_____

CREATIVE
INSPIRATIONS

"Just like the moon, we go through phases to reflect the light and the darkness within us."

RITUAL JOURNAL WORKSHEET

Phase Name : Write the name of the lunar phase (New Moon/Full Moon/Other)

_____

Date : Note the date of the phase.

_____

Intentions : What do you intend to manifest or release? Write in affirmative "I am ...." statements.

_____
_____
_____
_____
_____
_____
_____
_____
_____
_____

Moon Phase Meaning : Write down the meanings and symbolism associated with the lunar phase.

_____
_____
_____
_____

Ritual Practice : Describe the rituals you performed during this phase. Include any meditations, or ceremonies you engaged in.

_____

_____

_____

_____

_____

_____

Reflections : Reflect on your experiences, lessons learned and takeaways. How did you feel during, before and after the ritual? Did you notice any shifts or changes in your energy? Reflect on your emotions, mood and physical state during this lunar phase. How did you feel emotionally, mentally, physically and spiritually? Did you notice any changes in your energy levels, sleep patterns, or overall health? Did you receive any guidance or messages from your intuition, dreams, or spiritual practice? Write down three things that you are grateful for.

_____

_____

_____

_____

_____

_____

_____

_____

_____

_____

Next Steps : What are your next steps? Set intentions for the next lunar cycle.

_____

_____

_____

_____

_____

_____

_____

_____

_____

_____

Closing Blessings : Offer a blessing or affirmation to conclude your journal entry and sign it.

_____

_____

_____

_____

_____

_____

CREATIVE
INSPIRATIONS

"As the moon knows, it's the quiet energy that has the power to pull."

YOUR CORE VALUES

Circle the core values from that list,that most resonates with you:

Authenticity	Fame	Peace
Achievement	Friendships	Pleasure
Adventure	Fun	Poise
Authority	Growth	Popularity
Autonomy	Happiness	Recognition
Balance	Honesty	Religion
Beauty	Humor	Reputation
Boldness	Influence	Respect
Compassion	Inner Harmony	Responsibility
Challenge	Justice	Security
Citizenship	Kindness	Self-Respect
Community	Knowledge	Service
Competency	Leadership	Spirituality
Contribution	Learning	Stability
Creativity	Love	Success
Curiosity	Loyalty	Status
Determination	Meaningful Work	Trustworthiness
Fairness	Openness	Wealth
Faith	Optimism	Wisdom

THE MYSTICAL ALCHEMIST
WHEEL OF LIFE

Review the 8 categories, and If necessary rename category segments to add in something that is missing, or make it more meaningful to you. Write down your intentions in each area.

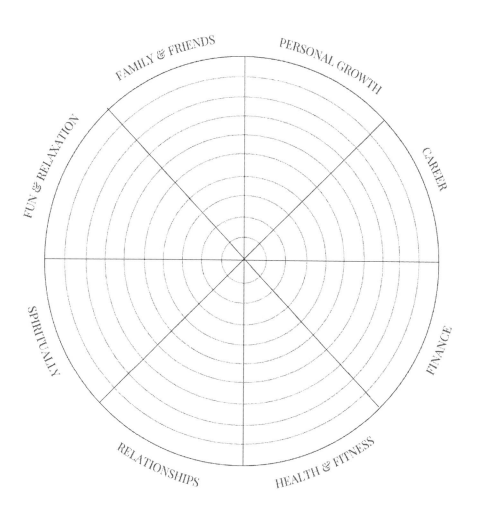

VISION ◈ PLANNER

Plan 3 main goals you have for next year. write them
down and the actions you will take to achieve them.

GOAL 1:	GOAL 2:	GOAL 3:
ACTIONS:	ACTIONS:	ACTIONS:

THE MYSTICAL ALCHEMIST
GOAL PLANNER

THE GOAL:

_____
_____
_____
_____
_____
_____
_____

THE STRATEGY:

_____
_____
_____
_____
_____
_____
_____

NEXT ACTIONS:

_____
_____
_____
_____

NOTES:

_____
_____
_____
_____

THE MYSTICAL ALCHEMIST
GOAL PLANNER

THE GOAL:

_____
_____
_____
_____
_____
_____
_____

THE STRATEGY:

_____
_____
_____
_____
_____
_____
_____

NEXT ACTIONS: NOTES:

_____   _____
_____   _____
_____   _____
_____   _____

THE MYSTICAL ALCHEMIST GOAL PLANNER

THE GOAL:

_____
_____
_____
_____
_____
_____
_____

THE STRATEGY:

_____
_____
_____
_____
_____
_____
_____

NEXT ACTIONS: NOTES:

_____   _____
_____   _____
_____   _____
_____   _____

THE MYSTICAL ALCHEMIST
GOAL PLANNER

THE GOAL:

_____

_____

_____

_____

_____

_____

_____

THE STRATEGY:

_____

_____

_____

_____

_____

_____

_____

NEXT ACTIONS: NOTES:

_____   _____

_____   _____

_____   _____

_____   _____

THE MYSTICAL ALCHEMIST GOAL PLANNER

THE GOAL:

_____
_____
_____
_____
_____
_____
_____

THE STRATEGY:

_____
_____
_____
_____
_____
_____

NEXT ACTIONS: NOTES:

_____   _____
_____   _____
_____   _____
_____   _____

THE MYSTICAL ALCHEMIST GOAL PLANNER

THE GOAL:

_____
_____
_____
_____
_____
_____
_____
_____

THE STRATEGY:

_____
_____
_____
_____
_____
_____
_____
_____

NEXT ACTIONS:

_____
_____
_____
_____

NOTES:

_____
_____
_____
_____

THE MYSTICAL ALCHEMIST
GOAL PLANNER

THE GOAL:

_____

_____

_____

_____

_____

_____

_____

THE STRATEGY:

_____

_____

_____

_____

_____

_____

_____

NEXT ACTIONS:

_____

_____

_____

_____

NOTES:

_____

_____

_____

_____

THE MYSTICAL ALCHEMIST GOAL PLANNER

THE GOAL:

_____

_____

_____

_____

_____

_____

_____

THE STRATEGY:

_____

_____

_____

_____

_____

_____

_____

NEXT ACTIONS: NOTES:

_____   _____

_____   _____

_____   _____

_____   _____

YOUR NOTES

Manifesting with the moon

YOUR NOTES:

Manifesting with the moon

YOUR NOTES

Manifesting with the moon

MOON RITUAL MASTERCLASS

Embark on a transformative journey and
immerse yourself in a world of lunar magic,
supported by a wealth of resources and a vibrant
community of fellow seekers.

MOON RITUAL MASTERCLASS

Illuminate Your Path with Priestess Heather Regal Salmon

Dive deeper into the enchanting world of lunar wisdom with our Moon Ritual Masterclass, featuring Priestess Heather Regal Salmon, renowned author, sound healer, ceremonialist and spiritual guide. But that's not all! When you enroll, you'll also gain access to an array of invaluable free bonuses and a vibrant community of like-minded souls.

Bonuses Include:

1. **Moon Phase Calendar:** Stay attuned to the celestial rhythms with our exclusive moon phase calendar, designed to help you track and optimize your rituals throughout the lunar cycle.

2. **Guided Sound Healing Meditations & Invocation:** Immerse yourself in the soothing embrace of guided meditations led by Heather Regal Salmon herself. These powerful audio journeys will deepen your connection to.the moon and awaken your inner wisdom.

3. **Workbook and Journaling Prompts:** Enhance your learning experience with a comprehensive workbook filled with insightful prompts and exercises to enrich your practice and integrate your newfound knowledge.

4. **Exclusive Discounts:** Enjoy special discounts on future courses, products, and events curated exclusively for members of our Moon Ritual Masterclass community.

Community Features

1. **Private Online Forum:** Where full and new moon updates and rituals are posted. Connect with fellow seekers, share experiences, and receive ongoing support in our private online forum. Engage in meaningful discussions, ask questions, and celebrate your journey with a community of kindred spirits.

2. **Live Q&A Sessions:** Gain further clarity and guidance from Heather Regal Salmon herself during live Q&A sessions exclusive to members. Deepen your understanding, address your queries, and receive personalized insights to enrich your practice.

3. **Virtual Ritual Circles:** Come together in virtual ritual circles to honor the moon, cultivate intention, and amplify the power of collective energy. Experience the magic of ritual in a supportive and inclusive environment.

4. **Guest Expert Workshops:** Expand your knowledge and explore related topics through guest expert workshops featuring leading voices in spirituality, wellness, and personal development.

Embark on this transformative journey and immerse yourself in a world of lunar magic, supported by a wealth of resources and a vibrant community of fellow seekers. Enroll now and join us as we illuminate the path to empowerment, enlightenment, and infinite possibility.

JOIN THE MASTERCLASS

THE AUTHORS

Heather and Donny Regal are the cofounders of the Black Swan Temple and Mystical Alchemy Sound Healing and are both ordained clergy of the Temple of Isis.

These innovative visionary mystics bring decades of experience as professional performers, healers, producers and agents of change. Heather and Donny, twin flames, have been together creatively and romantically since 2011 and reside at the Black Swan Temple, their beautiful nature sanctuary and farm in Maui, Hawaii.

They have produced over 30 Sound Healing CDs, authored the World Fusion Plant Based Recipe Book, created award winning inspiring short films, and offer sacred sound ceremonies, online mystery school initiations, personal transformative retreats, as well as sacred pilgrimages to ancient Egypt

Made in the USA
Columbia, SC
08 July 2024

38181447R00070